IS MOTHERHOOD AN *INSTITUTION*?

The Mother-Daughter Relationship in
George Eliot's *Scenes of Clerical Life*,
Sylvia Plath's *The Bell Jar*, and
Angela Carter's *The Bloody Chamber*

IS MOTHERHOOD AN *INSTITUTION?*

The Mother-Daughter Relationship in
George Eliot's *Scenes of Clerical Life*,
Sylvia Plath's *The Bell Jar,* and
Angela Carter's *The Bloody Chamber*

ELENA RECIO RUIZ

UCOPress
Editorial Universidad de Córdoba

Is Motherhood an *Institution*? The Mother-Daughter Relationship in George Eliot's *Scenes of Clerical Life*, Sylvia Plath's *The Bell Jar*, and Angela Carter's *The Bloody Chamber* – Córdoba: UCOPress. Editorial Universidad de Córdoba, 2024

14 x 21,5 cm, 88 pp.

THEMA: IBSF
Elena Recio Ruiz

N.º 5 de la colección de Estudios de Género Simone de Beauvoir

Directora de la colección: Silvia Medina Quintana

© Elena Recio Ruiz

© Edita: UCOPress. Editorial Universidad de Córdoba, 2024
Campus Universitario de Rabanales
Ctra. Nacional IV, Km 396. 14071 Córdoba (España)
Tel.: (+34) 957 212 165
https://ucopress.uco.es • ucopress@uco.es

ISBN: 978-84-9927-812-4
eISBN: 978-84-9927-813-1
DL: CO-1360-2024

Impresión: Gráficas Minerva de Córdoba, S.L.
Tel. 957 322 222

Impreso en papel ecológico

UCOPress (Cordoba University Press) is member of UNE, which guarantees the dissemination and commercialization of its publications at a national and international level.

Impreso en España

INDEX

1
INTRODUCTION

Motherhood and the mother-daughter relationship have been depicted through different ways in literature. On the one hand, in some narratives the mother has been described as an evil figure or as somebody who constricts the daughter's freedom and whose ideas the daughter tries to reject. While, on the other hand, motherhood has been conceived as an everlasting and unconditional feeling of love towards the children, portraying the mother as a caring and loving figure.

In this monograph,1 the mother-daughter relationship of three different narratives will be analysed, in order to examine if motherhood is presented in them, in Adrienne Rich's words, as an institution through which patriarchal values are maintained and indoctrinated from mothers to daughters. Thus, the diegeses which are going to be examined are a chapter of the work written by George Eliot, Scenes of Clerical Life, which was first published in 1857, titled "The Sad Fortunes of the Reverend Amos Barton"; the only ever written novel by the poet Sylvia Plath, The Bell Jar, dating from 1963; and

---

1   This monograph is the result of the research conducted in an Undergraduate Thesis of the English Studies degree at University of Córdoba. This thesis was supervised by Dr Juan de Dios Torralbo Caballero, and it was defended on the 23rd of June 2023.

the story "The Bloody Chamber" from The Bloody Chamber and Other Stories by Angela Carter, which dates from 1979. Consequently, the differences among these mother-daughter relationships will be studied considering the various decades in which these stories occur, the Victorian England of the 19th century, the 50s in the USA and the 70s respectively. Thereby, one of the main objectives of this monograph is to examine if the way such relationship is depicted has changed in literature. Moreover, the decision of choosing these three works is due to the fact that they present three different types of mothers, and of mother-daughter relationships, which at the end are shaped according to the social and gender standards of each of the times in which they are set. Since these three narratives provide with different types of motherhood, they were regarded as propitious to answer the question this study wants to respond from different perspectives, because as a matter of length this study could not compare more diegesis, in order to give more points of view, if it wanted to be concise2. In this way, on the one hand, this work analyses the mother-daughter relationship between Milly and Patty Barton in Eliot's "The Sad Fortunes of the Reverend Amos Barton", which is one of obedience, mildness and following the pattern of gender roles. On the other hand, it also examines the relationship between Mrs Greenwood and her daughter Esther from Plath's The Bell Jar, which is more ambiguous due to the time when is set and the social changes women are facing. Additionally, in this novel the daughter rejects the figure of the mother and becoming like her, breaking with previous patterns. Finally, this monograph

---

2   This monograph, being the result of an Undergraduate Thesis of the English Studies degree at University of Córdoba, followed its corresponding guidelines.

also analyses the mother-daughter relationship in Carter's "The Bloody Chamber" where the mother breaks free from gender norms and becomes the saviour of the daughter, who regards her mother as a role model instead of rejecting her.

1.1. Objectives

Hence, having in mind the question this study tries to answer, if motherhood in the aforesaid works functions as a patriarchal *institution*, through which conservative values and gender norms are instilled from mothers in daughters, this study has the following objectives:

1. To provide a theoretical framework in which the concepts used in this work are going to be explained in order to academically backup the analysis of the books that are going to be studied.

2. To briefly study the life and works of George Eliot to better comprehend the context of the work by her that is going to be analysed.

3. To briefly study the life and works of Sylvia Plath to better comprehend the context of the work by her that is going to be analysed.

4. To briefly study the life and works of Angela Carter to better comprehend the context of the work by her that is going to be analysed.

5. To carry out an analysis of motherhood and the mother-daughter relationship in the chosen narratives to answer the question this research poses.

6. To provide with the plot of "The Sad Fortunes of the Reverend Amos Barton" and its analysis, along

with a contextualisation of the time when this work is set.

7. To provide with the plot of *The Bell Jar* and its analysis, along with a contextualisation of the time when this work is set.

8. To provide with the plot of "The Bloody Chamber" and its analysis, along with a contextualisation of the time when this work is set.

9. To contrast these three mother-daughter relationships and draw conclusions answering the question this study poses.

Thus, objectives from five to nine are the main ones for this monograph, while objectives from one to four are secondary and work to achieve and back up the primary ones.

1.2. Methodology, Contents, and Structure

Then, in order to follow these objectives, this research was divided in different parts. In the first place, regarding the first objective, the theoretical framework of this study is found in the section entitled "1.3. Theoretical Framework: Mothers, Daughters, Gender, and *Institution*", which contains all the academic and theoretical backup of the monograph, explaining the different concepts that are used in its analysis. Thus, to write this section the sources that were studied the most are the books *Of Woman Born: Motherhood Experience and Institution* by Adrienne Rich and *The Mother/Daughter Plot: Narrative, Psychoanalysis and Feminism* by Marianne Hirsch, which constitute the theoretical backbone of this research. Furthermore, other sources were examined too, such as the Cambridge Dictionary to provide definitions of *motherhood, mother* and *daughter* as a starting point of this reflection upon maternity, together with Hala Ewaidat's article *Reconstructing the Mother-Daughter Relationship: Lydia Davis and Amy Tan* and Nel Noddings' *Caring: A Feminine Approach to Ethics & Moral Education* to provide with other definitions for motherhood. Moreover, the definitions given by Hirsch and Rich in the above-mentioned works were also mentioned. In this way, these different depictions of motherhood were discussed in "1.3.1. Defining Motherhood and the Mother-Daughter Relationship".

In the second place, in the section "1.3.2. The *Institution*: Shaping Women Through Maternity and *Gender Performativity*", once that Rich's concept of *institution* had been explained, together with her definition of motherhood, the origins of maternity as such patriarchal tool were examined thanks to what Hirsch proposes in her work cited above. What is more, what John Ruskin states in *Of Queens' Gardens*, along with Virginia Woolf's thoughts in *Professions for Women*, where she deals with the concept of the *Angel in the House*, and Coventry Patmore's notion of women in *The Angel in the House*, were studied to prove the origins of this *institution* Hirsch sets in the Victorian times are true. Next, the concept of *gender performativity* from Judith Butler's *Performative Acts and Gender Constitution: An Essay in Phenomenology and Feminist Theory* is explained to link gender norms with the repetition of the pattern established by the conception of motherhood as a patriarchal *institution*. Furthermore, this concept is chiselled under the *male gaze* Laura Mulvey deals with in *Visual and Other Pleasures*, also explained in this section.

In the third place, in the section "1.3.3. The Constricted Identity of the Mother and the Disidentification of the Daughter Through Matrophobia", along with the sources and concepts mentioned above, Eula Bis' perspective on motherhood and identity in "Of Institution Born", a foreword to Adrienne Rich's book here studied; the concepts of disidentification and matrophia, from Rich's work as well; and Adams' reflection on the mother-daughter relationship and identity in "Maternal Bonds: Recent Literature on Mothering" are explained too to comprehend the impact of such relationship in both the mother's and the daughter's identity. For instance, the mother usually experiences the feeling of blame, a notion also discussed in this section.

Continuing with the objectives of this research, objectives number two, three and four are covered in "2. On the Life and Literary Work of the Authors", which is divided in the following sections: "2.1. George Eliot", "2.2. Sylvia Plath" and "2.3. Angela Carter". Thus, to examine the life and work of the authors *The Cambridge Companion to George Eliot*, *George Eliot: Her Mind and Her Art* by Joan Bennett, *The Cambridge Companion to Sylvia Plath*, *Sylvia Plath* by Elisabeth Bronfen, the biography of Sylvia Plath in the web page of Smith College, "Sylvia Plath Special Collections Resources: About Sylvia Plath", *Angela Carter* by Lorna Sage and the British Library online section "Angela Carter" were consulted to carry out these objectives regarding the authors' biographies.

Then, concerning the analysis of the narratives this monograph studies, objectives from five to eight inclusive are found in the section "3. Analysis: Is Motherhood an *Institution* in the Chosen Narratives?", divided into "3.1. George Eliot: Patty and Milly Barton", "3.1.1. 'The Sad Fortunes of the Reverend Amos Barton'", "3.1.2. Analysis", "3.2. Sylvia Plath: Esther and Mrs Greenwood", "3.2.1. *The Bell Jar*", "3.2.2. Analysis", "3.3. Angela Carter: the Daughter and the Mother in a New Perception of Motherhood", "3.3.1. 'The Bloody Chamber'" and "3.3.2. Analysis". In this way, in these sections the plot of the works analysed is explained together with an in-depth analysis of the mother-daughter relationship and motherhood in these diegesis using the aforementioned concepts and sources.

Finally, and concerning the last objective of this study, in section "4. Conclusions" motherhood in the different narratives is compared and conclusions are drawn after the study and analysis this research has carried out. Then, in "5. Works cited", all the sources and prime texts used in this work found.

1.3. Theoretical Framework: Mothers, Daughters, Gender, and *Institution*

Accordingly, the aim of this study is to discern if motherhood is presented, according to Adrienne Rich, as an *institution* in the chosen literary pieces, and in order to do that, first, a theoretical framework will be presented. Secondly, the life and work of the authors will be briefly described, and thirdly, examples will be taken from three narratives to prove if the institutionalisation with which Rich deals in the theoretical framework, together with other concepts, proves true or not. Finally, from this analysis and comparison of the characters from different periods, conclusions will be drawn.

To carry out such analysis the theory proposed by Rich in her work *Of Woman Born: Motherhood Experience and Institution* will be applied to determine if motherhood works as a tool of patriarchy to alienate women and perpetuate its values throughout generations in the chosen narratives. In this way, the theoretical framework of this monograph will be composed of, along with other academic articles and sources, Rich's theory in her work, cited above, and Marianne Hirsch's book *The Mother/Daughter Plot: Narrative, Psychoanalysis and Feminism*. Moreover, the fragments to analyse will be examined considering concepts such as the *Angel in the House*, the gender roles, *gender performativity, male gaze*, disidentification, or *matrophobia*, which will be explained later.

1.3.1. *Defining Motherhood and the Mother-Daughter Relationship*

Firstly, if an analysis on motherhood and the mother-daughter relationship is to be provided such concepts need to be defined. According to the Cambridge Dictionary, motherhood is "the state or time of being a mother" (Cambridge Dictionary), a mother is "a female parent" (Cambridge Dictionary) and a daughter "a female child in relation to her parents" (Cambridge Dictionary). Nevertheless, these semantic meanings acquire different connotations in our society. For example, Hala Ewaidat in her article *Reconstructing the Mother-Daughter Relationship: Lydia Davis and Amy Tan* describes the mother-daughter relationship as "an extraordinary bond that transcends geographical, cultural, and ethnic boundaries and unites women of every race and a historical period when they write novels, short stories, and books" (325). Therefore, for Ewaidat such relationship is very significant, out of the ordinary, and a common topic in the literary work of female writers.

Moreover, Nel Noddings in *Caring: A Feminine Approach to Ethics & Moral Education* considers that "[f]or many women, motherhood is the single greatest source of strength for the maintenance of the ethical ideal" (130), and that when a woman has given birth "[a]lready she feels the likelihood of eternal love and tenderness toward her child" (130). Consequently, from this perspective motherhood is considered in a more traditional way as an everlasting source of love which is unconditional and unique, which only brings positive things for the mother, and which is even related to ethics and morality.

Meanwhile, Marienne Hirsch in *The Mother/Daughter Plot: Narrative, Psychoanalysis, Feminism* points out that "[m]others the ones who are not singular, who did succumb to convention inasmuch as they are mothers—thereby become the targets of [a] process of disidentification and the primary negative models for the daughter" (11). In this statement motherhood is not described as a source of selfless love anymore, but as a constriction of the daughter's identity since mothers can incarnate "conventional constructions of femininity" (12), which the daughter might want to reject, as it will be later analysed. Such conventions, according to Hirsch, are what the heroine of 19th century, modernists, and post-modernists stories avoid, along with "conventional heterosexual romance and marriage plots" (11).

What is more, Adrienne Rich highlights two different definitions of motherhood in her work *Of Woman Born: Motherhood Experience and Institution*. On the one hand, Rich talks about the "the *potential relationship* of any woman to her powers of reproduction and to children" (lxi); and, on the other hand, she deals with the conception of motherhood as an *institution*, "the *institution*, which aims at ensuring that that potential—an all women—shall remain under control" (lxi). Thus, from Rich's perspective, motherhood is proclaimed as an *institution* through which patriarchal values are perpetuated and repeated. In this way, women, mothers, the ones who "did succumb to convention" (Hirsch 11) are alienated to reproduce in their daughters the same social patterns with which they have been indoctrinated since they had been raised up in and by a patriarchal society. In Rich's words, motherhood "has alienated women from our bodies by incarcerating us in them" (lxi).

Hence, the perception of motherhood has been changing through the decades and this has also been reflected in literature. Motherhood has been seen as a crucial moment of a woman's life, something women needed to achieve to be considered fully a woman in the eyes of society. Otherwise, they were rejected and called "barren", or they felt guilty if they were not able to give birth, as it is the case of the protagonist of the play *Yerma* written by Federico García Lorca in 1934. Moreover, not to become a mother can even imply being an "unwoman". For instance, in the dystopian novel written by Margaret Atwood, *The Handmaid's Tale*, being pregnant is crucial to survive for certain women, who are only valued due to their reproductive capacity.

This study focuses on Rich's and Hirsch's perspectives on motherhood, particularly on Rich's, though it also takes into account previous perceptions of motherhood, since they shape the mother figure that embodies tradition, and which is rejected by daughters in some fictions. To carry out the analysis of the three above-mentioned narratives, "The Sad Fortunes of the Reverend Amos Barton", *The Bell Jar*, and "The Bloody Chamber", along with the *institution* of motherhood, other concepts will be considered, such as *gender performativity*, the *male gaze*, the blame of the mothers, the identity of both mothers and daughters, the *Angel in the house*, and the idea of *matrophobia*.

1.3.2. *The Institution: Shaping Women through Maternity and Gender Performativity*

As it has been explained before, according to Rich, maternity can be erected as an *institution*, in order to control women and preserve patriarchal ideas through generations. Inasmuch as society's thoughts are embedded in us, maternity involves a preconception for women about how they should feel, think, and behave. For instance, mothers are expected to love their children selflessly, and in an eternal and unconditional way, just like Noddings points out, a mother should feel "eternal love and tenderness toward her child" (130). Nonetheless, Rich states that there are "unexamined assumptions" (3) regarding maternity, and that:

> A 'natural' mother is a person without further identity, one who can find her chief gratification in being all day with small children, living at a pace tuned to theirs; that the isolation of mothers and children together in the home must be taken for granted. (Rich 3)

Therefore, traditionally it was thought that a woman could not feel more gratified or fulfilled than being all the time with her children, taking care of them and loving them, at home, being relegated to the domestic sphere. Hence, the idea of maternity that patriarchal society had instilled in the author made her feel as if she "was haunted by the stereotype of the mother whose love is 'unconditional'; and by the visual and literary images of motherhood as a single-minded identity" (7), because "women—above all, mothers—have been supposed to love this way" (7).

However, such expectations on mothers, and women in general, which, as Rich claims are "taken for granted" (7), have an origin. Marianne Hirsch points out in her book *The Mother/Daughter Plot: Narrative, Psychoanalysis, Feminism* that "[t]he ideology of motherhood as the ideal femininity coincides with the institutionalization of childhood during the eighteenth and nineteenth centuries" (14). During this period, the images of "child's vulnerability and need for nurturing and protection" (Hirsch 14) were recurrent, which shaped the conception of maternity into "an 'instinct' and a 'natural' role and form of human connection, as well as a practice" (Hirsch 14). Moreover, given the historical context of the industrialisation, "[t]he private sphere was isolated from the public under industrial capitalism" (Hirsch 14) and "women became identified with and enclosed within the private sphere" (Hirsch 14). Thereby, "[i]n a largely technological and impersonal public world, motherhood … became the force of conservation of traditional values" (Hirsch 14).

Thus, the *institution* which Rich sets out finds its origins, as Hirsch explains, in the 18th and 19th centuries. What is more, the ideals described by Hirsch were backed up by many thinkers at that time, such as John Ruskin in the Victorian era, period in which the first work to be analysed, by George Eliot, is set. Thus, such ideals have been inherited from mothers to daughters through the decades, since they imply the mould in which women were supposed to fit in. In this way, Ruskin encourages the women of his time to fit in the mould of domesticity, postulating in his work *Of Queens' Gardens* that:

> The man's power is active, progressive, defensive. He is eminently the doer, the creator, the discoverer, the defender. His intellect is for speculation and invention; his energy for adventure, for war, and for conquest, wherever was is just, wherever conquest necessary. But the woman's power is for rule, not for battle,—and her intellect is not for invention or creation, but for sweet ordering, arrangement, and decision. (158)

These ideas from the Victorian times prove that "women have not been makers and sayers of patriarchal culture" (Rich lix) but rather passive subjects. Likewise, such thoughts are linked to the concept of the "ideal family" of this period, together with the above-mentioned concepts of "ideal femininity" (Hirsch 14) and the private sphere to which women, and mothers, were reduced. What is more, in relation to this, Ruskin also states that:

> [T]he man, in his rough work in open world, must encounter all peril and trial ... [b]ut he guards the woman from all this; within his house, as ruled by her, unless she herself has sought it, need enter no danger, no temptation, no cause of error or offense". (158)

Consequently, this fragment shows that "women became identified with and enclosed within the private sphere" (Hirsch 14). Hence, due to the fact that in the Victorian era women were associated to the domestic field, it was thought that:

> This is true nature of home—it is the place of Peace; the shelter, not only from all injury, but from all terror, doubt, and division. In so far as it is not this, it is not home: so far as the anxieties of the outer life penetrate into it, and the inconsistentlyminded, unknown, unloved, or hostile society of the outer world is allowed by either husband or wife to cross the threshold, it ceases to be home. (Ruskin 158-59)

Thereby, this excerpt proves that Victorian society regarded women, and mothers, as beings belonging to the interior, the home, the house, the domestic and the private sphere, since it was considered that, in Ruskin's words, "wherever a true wife comes, this home is always round her" (159). Therefore, the citation above quoted by Rich, "that the isolation of mothers and children together in the home must be taken for granted" (3), made in the 70s, proves its relation to the values instilled and perpetuated since the 18th century; which, as it will be later shown in the analysis of the literary works, are preserved throughout the generations from mothers to daughters, thanks to the institutionalisation of motherhood that Rich points out. For instance, reminiscences of these thoughts from the 18th century, present in "The Sad Fortunes of the Reverend Amos Barton" by Eliot, are found in *The Bell Jar* by Plath, as it will be later analysed.

What is more, in relation to how women (and mothers) are described by Ruskin and shaped by Victorian society, there is another concept which is going to be taken into account when analysing some of the works this monograph is concerned with, the *Angel in the House*. Virginia Woolf uses this term, which comes from a collection of poems named under the same title written by Coventry Patmore, dating from 1854 and 1862. In his work the English poet expresses the importance of home and constitutes the traits of the ideal Victorian woman. This book of poems shows the mould women had to fit in during Victorian times. For instance, some of the lines such as "[s]he was so gentle and so good" (Patmore 27) or "[t]he lack of lovely pride, in her/ Who strives to please, my pleasure numbs" (Patmore 28), proves what Woolf highlights in *Professions for Women*. In her work Woolf uses this symbol of the *Angel in the House* to explain the difficulties she faced when writing and carrying out her professional career, pointing out that such preconception about women constitutes an obstacle for them and for herself. In this way, Woolf explains that the *Angel in the House* "was intensely sympathetic. She was immensely charming. She was utterly unselfish. She excelled in the difficult arts of family life. She sacrificed herself daily" (141); and that "in short she was so constituted that she never had a mind or a wish of her own, but preferred to sympathize always with the

minds and wishes of others. Above all—I need not say it—
she was pure" (141). In this way, such conception of women
represents a hurdle for Woolf's job as a writer, since she felt
constricted when it came to write her fictional production,
because she was expected to behave, act, think and express
herself in a certain way. Likewise, Virginia Woolf highlights
the idea that the *Angel in the House* "never had a mind or
a wish of her own" (141), which Rich points out when
talking about motherhood and the way it constricts women's
identity. This is seen when Rich expresses that her view on
maternity has been narrowed by "the visual and literary
images of motherhood" (7), which presents it as involving
a "single-minded identity" (7). Thereby, the constriction
in women's identity when becoming a mother, with which
Rich deals in her work, is also related to the limits set on
women in the previous centuries, the moulds Ruskin and
Woolf depicted. Thus, mothers have set the same boundaries
for their daughters through the years, repeating the same
pattern, wanting their daughters to fit in the same mould, the
same stereotype they thought they should accomplish. This
perpetuation of traditional ideas throughout the *institution*
of motherhood has been portrayed in literature as Rich
claims when talking about those "visual and literary images
of motherhood" (7) which, by depicting the society of the
time when they were written, have helped to reinforce these
values, as it will be exemplified later through excerpts of
George Eliot's writing. This is why, Woolf poses that "[k]
illing the Angel in the House was part of the occupation of
a woman writer" (142), since accepting what this concept
means implies denying one's critical thinking and freedom
as a woman.

Thereby, Patmore's *Angel in the House* embodies the
epitome of the ideal Victorian woman, which is also described

by Ruskin, as shown above. Interestingly, women's role is defined by two male authors, in this case, which means that is chiselled under a *male gaze*. As Laura Mulvey outlines in her work *Visual and Other Pleasures*:

> [I]n a world ordered by sexual imbalance, pleasure in looking has been split between active/male and passive/female. The determining male gaze projects its fantasy onto the female figure, which is styled accordingly. (19)

In this way, the ideal woman proposed by above-mentioned Victorian thinkers is "styled accordingly" (Mulvey 19) their wishes, male wishes, patriarchal ones, which is why they attribute women qualities such as being mild, subdued, tender, empathetic, gentle, good, unselfish or pure, not having "a mind of her own" (Woolf 141). Thus, patriarchy perpetuates certain traits in women through gender roles to have power over them and to reinforce the "conservation of traditional values" (Hirsch 14). This is why, as it has been mentioned above, when it comes to women and motherhood, there are particular ideas about women which come from back in history, such as the ones from the Victorian era, that have been rooted in society. Such thoughts have overcome many decades, and have had a lot of influence, as the work written by Rich in the decade of the 70s proves, since it highlights expectations on mothers that date back to decades ago. Indeed, one of the main reasons why such values have overcome the pass of time is the institutionalisation of motherhood Rich talks about. Throughout maternity, mothers who were alienated by the Angel in the House and traditionally wanted to keep conventions in order to fit in their society raised their daughters with such ideals and instilled in them these values. This fact will be studied later, particularly in two of the works to be analysed: "The Sad Fortunes of the Reverend Amos Barton", dating precisely from the Victorian era, and The Bell Jar, which, even if it is set in the 50s, brings to light the perpetuation of patriarchal thoughts and gender roles over the years.

Finally, linked to the concepts that have been just explained of *Angel in the House* and the *male gaze*, which will be further analysed through excerpts of the literary works chosen for this study, the notion of *gender performativity* needs to be examined. According to the American philosopher Judith Butler, in her work *Performative Acts and Gender Constitution: An Essay in Phenomenology and Feminist Theory*, humans are not born with a particular gender, but rather perform and repeat certain acts that are regarded in our society as feminine or masculine, and in this way, this ends up constructing our identity. Thus, Butler postulates that:

> When Simone de Beauvoir claims, "one is not born, but, rather, becomes a woman," she is appropriating and reinterpreting this doctrine of constituting acts from the phenomenological tradition. In this sense, gender is in no way a stable identity or locus of agency from which various acts proceede; rather, it is an identity tenuously constituted in time—an identity instituted through a stylized repetition of acts. (519)

Therefore, Butler's theory, which will be also applied in the literary analysis later on, proves what was stated above on the construction of women's roles, and on the ideal *Angel in the House* as a concept created by and under society's *male gaze*. In this sense, this role, in relation to mothers particularly, being this the main topic of this monograph, has remained all along history thanks to the "stylized repetition of acts" (Butler 519). This implies that, since women have tended to perform their gender role, then, as mothers, they have also played according to what was expected of them by society and, what is more, they have handed over these expectations to their daughters. Then, since mothers belong to a patriarchal society and are embedded in it, in some narratives they become an *institution* which is to maintain patriarchal values through repetition, throughout the "stylized repetition of acts" (Butler 519), as it will be seen in some of the works that will be examined later.

1.3.3. The Constricted Identity of the Mother and the Disidentification of the Daughter through Matrophobia

Gender roles and *gender performativity* define men's and women's identity, since they act according to what is expected from their gender and, therefore, this fact constricts them. Thus, it has been believed all along history that for women to fulfil their womanhood, and to act according to their gender, they needed to become mothers. As it was mentioned before, women who could not bear a child were labelled as 'barren' or 'unwoman', in this sense, maternity defines and limits women, and as a result their identity. Likewise, Rich poses that "[w] oman's status as a childbearer has been made into a major fact of her life. Terms like 'barren' or 'childless' have been used to negate any further identity. The term 'nonfather' does not exist in any realm of social categories" (lx). Consequently, becoming a mother clearly chisels women's identity, while the one of men is not shaped in this way since, traditionally, they are not pressured in the same way to become fathers and they are not expected to show in the same way as mothers an unconditional and everlasting love towards their children. Their expectations and its differences depend on their gender, according to which both parts tend to perform.

The American writer Eula Biss, in a foreword to Rich's *Of Woman Born: Motherhood Experience and Institution*, reflects upon such expectations and becoming a mother: "I had always feared what becoming a mother might do to me, and even after having a baby, I feared losing myself to motherhood" (xii). Moreover, Eula Biss also explains that what she "[w]as resisting was becoming a role, rather than a person" (xii). In Rich's words, Biss "didn't want to enter the institution of motherhood" (xii). Thereby, becoming a mother means for some women that "[w]hatever her choice, her body [will] under[go] irreversible changes, her mind will never be the same, her future as a woman has been shaped by the event" (Rich lx). What is more, Rich points out that:

> Motherhood, in the sense of an intense, reciprocal relationship with a particular child, or children, is *one part* of female process; it is not an identity. The housewife in her mid-fourties may jokingly say, "I feel like someone out of job." But in the eyes of society, once having been mothers, what are we if not always mothers? (18-19)

Accordingly, the incompatibility of being a mother and having an own identity seems not to be feasible if one follows society's assumptions, given the context when this work is written, the 70s. What is more, this situation even remains in the same way for some women nowadays. In this way, motherhood has reduced not only women's identity but also their opportunities, since, as Rich highlights "motherhood as an institution has ghettoized and degraded female potentialities" (lxi). Thereby, like Rich suggests:

> Under patriarchy, female possibility has been literally massacred on the site of motherhood. Most women in history have become mothers without choice, and even greater number have lost their lives bringing life into the world. (lxi-lxii)

Gender roles and *gender performativity* work to shape one's identity, in a way that becoming a mother might be limiting for women. Moreover, such gender expectations, as seen above are "styled accordingly" (Mulvey 19) by society and, living in a patriarchal one, this implies that gender roles have been constituted to keep on with tradition, in order to preserve the power in male hands. Thus, motherhood becomes a tool of patriarchy when it makes of it an *institution*, due to the fact that it is seen as "the force of conservation of traditional values" (Hirsch 14). Women in some narratives had participated in the institutionalisation because of the alienation they have suffered, since they were raised according to patriarchal values as well, which they were taught to repeat and perform.

In addition, the concept of blame is often found in the literature written about mothers. For instance, they often blame themselves or are blamed if they do not live up to society's expectations has of them: when their children do not stick to the path they are believed to follow, then they have been considered a "bad mother"; if they are not able to get pregnant, they have been called "barren"; or if they do not feel as they think they should, according to society, when becoming mothers they have been regarded as "anti-women". For example, in her book, Rich also shares her personal experience when becoming a mother, when she often blamed herself because she "was haunted by the stereotype of the mother whose love is 'unconditional'; and by the visual and literary images of motherhood as a single-minded identity" (3). In fact, the author even claims that "[p]erhaps one is a monster—an anti-woman—something driven and without recourse to the normal and appealing consolations of love, motherhood" (2) when she feels guilty because she does not fit in the stereotyped mould of being a "good" or "perfect" mother. Rich states too that she felt that her "fate … is to serve a function for which I was not fitted" (1), and that she envied "the barren woman who has the luxury of her regrets but lives a life of privacy and freedom" (1). These thoughts of blame and guilt also bring to life the alienation in which women are embedded, thinking they have to fulfil patriarchy's expectations and feeling like a failure if they do not achieve them.

In the excerpt quoted above, Rich poses that motherhood is presented, like it has been mentioned previously, as a "single-minded identity" (3), and this is due to the fact that "[w]oman's status as childbearer has been made into a major fact of her life" (lix-lx) by society. In this way, when women want to accomplish their role according to patriarchy, since "women have not been makers and sayers of patriarchal culture" (Rich lix), but have been alienated by it, they become a patriarchal *institution* for their daughters, as Rich highlights:

> [I]t is the mother through whom patriarchy early teaches the small female her proper expectations. The anxious pressure of one female on another to conform to a degrading and dispiriting role can hardly be termed "mothering", even if she does this believing it will help her daughter to survive. (250)

Consequently, the mother becomes for the daughter "a pattern of repetition from which she cannot emerge and which precludes further development and progression" (Hirsch 21). Accordingly, this is why daughters in some narratives tend to reject their mothers and they do not regard them as role models, since they incarnate patriarchal constrictions of the self and conservative values, as it is the case of the mother-daughter relationship in *The Bell Jar*, which will be analysed later. Thereby, for the daughter to shape her own identity sometimes she needs to separate from the mother, to reject her principles, in short, she undergoes a process of disidentification from the mother and the "maternal dominance" (Hirsch 20). Such rejection is coined by the poet Lynn Sukenick as *matrophobia*, which like Rich points out in her book "is the fear not of one's mother but of *becoming one's mother*" (240). Hence, this concept and process of disidentification is a way for the daughter to create an identity of her own:

> [T]housands of daughters see their mothers as having taught a comprise and self-hatred they are struggling to win free of, the one through whom the restrictions and degradations of female experience were perforce transmitted.(240)

Therefore, this excerpt proves the results of women's alienation in a society which teaches women to hate themselves, to undervalue their capacities and to stick to the gender norms, indoctrinating such values over and over again, when mothers put such ideas in the daughters' mind, which is why, as Rich postulates:

> Matrophobia can be seen as a womanly splitting of the self, in the desire to become purged once and for all of our mothers' bondage, to become individual and free. The mother stands for the victim in ourselves, the unfree woman, the martyr. Our personalities seem dangerously to blur and overlap with our mothers'; and in a desperate attempt to know where mother ends and daughter begins, we perform radical surgery. (242)

Thereby, in some narratives, daughters "are infuriated either because they see their mothers as pressuring them to conform to their own or society's expectations of girls and women or because they find their mothers disdaining those expectations" (Ewaidat 325). This is due to, as mentioned before, "the external and internalized social pressures to relate and accept responsibilities to and for each other in terms of the culturally defined roles of mothers and daughters" (Ewaidat 325). Then, this is the reason why in some literary works, as Adams states:

> Mothers are discussed as a source of anger and emotional pain for their children, especially daughters. Most treatments of mothering, feminist or not, emphasized that the primary task of the prototypical middle-class daughter was to separate. The choice that daughters seemed to face was either to reject Mom or to replicate what was identified as her limited identity as homemaker, her economic dependence on men, her annoying and fruitless attempts to live through her children, her years of thankless, stultifying service as wife and mother, and especially her lack of a sense of individual self-worth, the result of her oppression. (414)

Such rejection is often found in 19th century narratives, like Jane Austen's, for example, where mothers and daughters tend to be presented in an antagonistic way, as it is the case of the heroine of *Pride and Prejudice* and her mother. Therefore, Hirsch argues that:

> [I]n conventional nineteenth-century plots of the European and American tradition, the fantasy that controls the female family romance is the desire for the heroine's singularity based on disidentification from the fate of other women, especially mothers. (10)

What is more, Hirsch also believes that "the nineteenth-century heroine, determined to shape a different plot for herself, tends not only to be separated from the figure and the story of the mother, but herself tries to avoid maternity at all costs" (14). Meanwhile, in narratives from "Euro-American popular culture in the twentieth century … mother-daughter relationships were often represented as destructive" (Adams 419).

The relationship with her mother proves decisive for the daughter's life and development, since "according to bonding theory, the mother's success or failure in forging a strong bond with her newborn is directly responsible for the presence or absence of such problems in the lives of infants and children, but she is a passive rather than an active agent" (Adams 415). This is why "Prince (2020) asserts that girls find it difficult to break away from the overpowering influence of the mother. This, sometimes, hinders the girls from developing a normal sense of self, which affects their entire life" (Ewaidat 326).

Then, as it was claimed at the beginning of this monograph, the mother-daughter relationship has been presented in literature in several ways, such as an antagonistic one. Considering the above explained concepts of *matrophobia* and *institution*, along with the other ideas explained, an analysis of excerpts from the chosen narratives will be provided in order to answer the question which occupies this study, whether motherhood is presented as an institution in the selected plots or not.

To sum up, the *institution* that motherhood incarnates and preserves patriarchal values instilling traditional ideals from mothers in daughters throughout history. In this way, maternity shapes both the mother's and the daughter's identity, and the latter tries to create her own one sometimes through rejection and *matrophobia*. What is more, these concepts are shaped by *gender performativity* and gender roles, which in the end are created under the *male gaze*, in short by patriarchy. The creation of such concepts works just like the institutionalisation of motherhood, as another way to preserve the power in male hands by creating a passive stereotyped mould, like the *Angel in the House*, in which women are taught and believed to fit in. Thus, in this research excerpts from the chosen works will be examined to determine if maternity works as an *institution* in them. Moreover, in order to do that, the mother-daughter relationship in the three stories will be analysed according to the other concepts above explained to carry out an in-depth study and draw conclusions.

2
ON THE LIFE AND LITERARY
WORK OF THE AUTHORS

2.1. George Eliot

Mary Anne Evans, best known for her pen name George Eliot and her other many pseudonyms all along her life and career, was born on 22nd November 1819 in Warwickshire, England, child of the marriage of Robert Evans and Christiana Pearson. Mary Anne would spend her childhood in Griff House having a rural, farming and religious background that would very much affect her personal life and her literature later on. Indeed, although her family were not genteel, "it was [a] respectable and ambitious [family] of practical excellence within the terms of a conservative, customary rural society" (Bodenheimer 21). Such background would cause many arguments between the writer and her father during her youth due to the fact that religious and social constrictions clashed with the critical thoughts Mary Anne started to develop. Even if during her teenage years, when she studied in the local schools in Nuneaton and Coventry, the author shared the religious beliefs of her surroundings, which are expressed in the remaining correspondence with her friend Maria Lewis, soon she would show her own dissident opinion about them. At the age of sixteen, when her mother passes away and her sister Chrissey gets married, she starts taking care of the household, her father and her brother. Moreover, it is during this period of her more religious years when she self imposes herself repression and rejects earthly pleasures such as reading novels or playing music (Bodenheimer 22) and decides to drop "the "e" from "Anne," possibly to signal the rejection of an unnecessarily elegant frill" (Bodenheimer 22). Nonetheless, in her twenties her ideas started to change and in her exchange of letters with Maria Lewis she begins posing a critique to religion which was a result of her many readings and questioning. Mary Ann's reflections end up in the refusal of going to the church with her father, which would start an episode of many arguments in the Evans family, above all between father and daughter, which has been designated as the "Holy War". Furthermore, during this climate of criticism the writer meets a matrimony who would prove essential for the developing of Ann's critical thinking, the Brays, who would provide her with an atmosphere in which she could express herself and share her ideas freely. Afterwards, due to her new way of thinking and her refusal to go to church, her friendship with Maria Lewis ceased and after some more familial arguments among daughter, father, and brother, and staying for a while in in her brother's home, the "Holy War" came to a truce. In this way, Mary Ann decided to go back to live in Foleshill with her father, attend the church with him and hide her intellectual activity and friendship with the Brays, playing "to the full her role as devoted spinster daughter to Robert Evans" (Bodenheimer 25) until her father's death caused by an illness in 1848. Consequently, this event implies a radical change for the author, who completely took care of his father, and who "effectively abandoned her mental life and became his full-time nurse for a year, dedicating herself to this thankless task with all the passion of sacrifice that could have been asked of a fully licensed Victorian angel in the sickroom" (Bodenheimer 25). Therefore, when Robert Evans passes away, being the author thirty years old then, this gives her the freedom when thinking and expressing herself Ann had always longed for. Then, a year after her father's death, in 1849, Ann begins her life as an independent woman and, since thanks to the Brays she had previously been acquainted with radical intellectual circles. For instance, by translating German works on a criticism of religion for the publisher John Chapman, she moved into his household for liberal intellectuals in London. During this period of her life her name suffers another metamorphosis when Mary Ann decides to call herself "Marian" this time. Once in London, in 1851, Marian started to work as an assistant editor for Chapman's liberal journal *Westminster Review,* running it herself after Chapman's editorship until 1853, always under the anonymity who ensured her intellectual activity, freedom and success, due to the social constrictions her gender entailed (Bodenheimer 26). In this period of her life, her figure was a respectable one among the liberal freethinkers of London and other than running the journal she also wrote articles and reviews, though always under anonymity since "[o]fficially under cover, her gender was no impediment to the full exercise of her talents" (Bodenheimer 26). Later, in her midthirties, she met the writer, editor, and intellectual, George Henry Lewes, with whom she had "many opinions and tastes in common and used to go for country excursions together, discussing philosophy" (Bennett 53), a person who proved essential in her literary production and with whom she fall in love. Her relationship with Lewes involves her again in social criticism and gossip, just like in her "Holy War" years, because Lewes could not marry Marian legally since he was consenting the adultery of the woman he had married and with whom he had had children, Angew Jervis Lewes, and even had register four illegitimate children she had under his own name. Of course, the religious Victorian society of that time proved very sceptical about Marian and Lewes' relationship, which did not prevent them living together and having a loving relationship. After living together in 1854 in Berlin, they came back to London where Marian had to dealt with her professional career and being regarded as a "fallen woman" (Bodenheimer 28) in the eyes of Victorian social and gender standards. Even her brother Isaac cut the familial bonds off with her. It is during this time when Marian wanted to be known as "Marian Evan Lewes", "Marian Lewes" and "Mrs Lewes". After fruitfully writing numerous reviews in 1856 she writes her first piece of fictional writing, *The Sad Fortunes of the Reverend Amos Barton* (1857), which was later published together with two other novellas in *Scenes of Clerical Life* (Bodenheimer 29). Lewes always supported Marian and encouraged her to write, and also acted as a mediator between her partner and the publisher John Blackwood, who published all along her career Marian's novels under her pen name "George Eliot". This pseudonym allowed her once more the anonymity which ensure her a profession, freedom, and literary success. Nevertheless, again the rumours and gossip around her pen name tormented the author, especially since *Scenes of Clerical Life* (1857) and her most successful work *Adam Bede* (1859) recalled her infancy in Warwickshire. In this way, the neighbours of this rural area started rumours about a poor clergyman, who knew the true events on which the fiction was based, called Joseph Liggins, who they claimed was the writer behind George Eliot's persona. However, the couple had to ignore the rumours passed by since Marian's publisher fear the sales would drop if people knew about George Eliot's true identity and gender. Afterwards, Marian publishes *The Mill on the Floss* (1860), being the decade of the 1860s more experimental in terms of her writing. Nonetheless, even if she now was famous and had financial stability, during her forties she suffered from anxiety and depression (Bodenheimer 31). The writer undertook other literary projects which entailed more difficulties such as *Romola* (1863), *The Spanish Gypsy* (1868) and *Felix Holt, the Radical* (1866). By this time both partners started facing some hurdles regarding health that harden their work, such as Marian's headaches. On the other hand, in 1860 she has to take on her role as the stepmother of one of Lewes' son, Charles, once he is back from studying abroad. Eliot shared some hobbies and had a good relationship with him, "[m]ore importantly, the pleasures and trials of substitute parenthood entered fully into her psychological experience, and into the fiction she would produce for the rest of her writing life" (Bodenheimer 32). Then, Charles married and moved out and the two other sons of Lewes, Thornton, whom Marian nursed while he was ill, and Hebert, died because of an illness. Consequently, due to her role as a stepmother Marian, or George Eliot, felt more legitimate in the strange familial situation of the Lews and felt she accomplished the duties or the role of a full Victorian woman (Bodenheimer 33). During the last years of George Eliot's life, she writes *Middlemarch* in 1872 and *Daniel Deronda* 1876, considered as two of her best works. This success in the last period of her life made her enjoy finally the social respectability she had long for all along her life, being invited to social gatherings and even by friends in Oxford and Cambridge. Additionally, "[f]or the younger generation in particular, George Eliot was a revered figure of liberal wisdom who promised the kind of sympathetic understanding manifested by the narrators of her books" (Bodenheimer 34) to the point of taking "special pains to cultivate the friendship and the confidences of her younger admirers, who sometimes became substitutes for the family she did not have" (Bodenheimer 34). In 1878 George Henry Lewes dies because of a stomach cancer and in 1880 she marries John Walter Cross, with whom she could be part in a legal way of a respectable family and have someone who could take care of her remaining literature (Bodenheimer 36). Marian died on the same year due to a kidney disease and John published her letters and journals in 1885, preserving his wife's name and figure as a respectable writer. Finally, "[o]f all the pen names adopted by Victorian writers, George Eliot's is the one that has proven the most enduring, the one that did not fade away once the gender and identity of the author became known" (Bodenheimer 20).

2.2. Sylvia Plath

The American poet and writer Sylvia Plath was born in Boston, Massachusetts, on 27th October 1932. Her parents were Aurelia Schober and Otto Emil Plath, the former had Austrian origins and the latter, who was a University Professor of Biology in Boston, German roots although he had lived in Poland (Bronfen vii). In 1935, when her brother Warren is born, Sylvia Plath's family moves to Winthrop, in Massachusetts. Five years later, when Sylvia was eight years old, her father died after he had a leg amputated due to diabetes, which has been regarded as an event that left a mark on Sylvia's childhood. Then, in 1942, the family moves to Wellesley where the writer's mother starts working as a teacher in a High School. It is in this city where Sylvia attended public schools and began writing her first poetry and short stories with which she even won some contests (Bronfen vii).

Afterwards, in 1951 she starts studying in Smith College, a private and liberal university for women. Sylvia had a great career academically speaking, she participated in numerous organisations and university journals and magazines, such as the *Daily Hampshire Gazette*, the *Springfield Daily News*, and the *Campus Cat*. Furthermore, in 1952 she wins one of the two prices of the magazine *Mademoiselle* fiction contest, and a year later she is chosen, together with other American college students, to work in New York during the summer as a guest editor in this magazine (Bronfen vii). This experience affected her mental health deeply and when Sylvia went back home she attempted committing suicide, which is why Sylvia was later "hospitalized at the psychiatric clinic in Belmont, Massachusetts" (Bronfen vii). All these events were described with fictional tones in her only ever written novel *The Bell Jar*, which will be discussed later in the analysis of this monograph. However, she comes back to Smith college to finish her studies. Plath had a brilliant academic record and, for instance, in 1954 she was granted a scholarship to study the German language at the Harvard Summer School (Smith College). Finally, she graduates in 1955 with *summa cum laude* and having won prizes for poetry. What is more, Plath is awarded a Fulbright Fellowship to study at Cambridge. Thus, in 1956 she meets the poet Ted Hughes in England, whom she marries on 16th June the same year. A year later the matrimony goes to the USA and Plath stars working at Smith College. During the first years of marriage the couple dedicates their time to poetry and literature and travels around the country, but in 1959 they decide to move to London. In 1960 Sylvia gives birth to her first child, Frieda Rebecca, and in October of the same year she publishes her first collection of poems *The Colossus and Other Poems*. A year later, the poet suffers a miscarriage and an appendectomy and later the family moves to Devon. Afterwards, in 1962 the marriage has another child, Nicholas Farrar. During this same year Plath and Hughes separate and the former moves to London with her children (Bronfen viii). Then, a year later, in January 1963, Plath publishes the above-mentioned novel *The Bell Jar* under the pseudonym Victoria Lucas, and a month later, on the 11th of February, Plath commits suicide. "Her *Ariel* poems were published posthumously by Faber and Faber in 1965, and her *Collected Poems* (1981) won the Pulitzer Prize in 1982" (Smith College). Other works published after the death of the poet are *Johnny Panic and the Bible of Dreams* (1877) and *Mary Ventura and the Ninth Kingdom* (2019).

Sylvia Plath's work and poetry have been highly influential for the generations who came after her, in Wagner-Martin's words, "[t]o consider the effect of Sylvia's Plath writing on today's poetry scene is to marvel at the endurance of her poems" (52). In addition, regarding her influence, Entwistle's point out that:

> Surely, to make any kind of mark on posteriority, a poet can only be a 'powerful individual' … their influence is better judged by the ways in which any example can be shown to anchor, and/or resonate in the work of 'powerfully individual poets' who emerge in his or her wake. There seems to be little doubt that without Plath, late twentieth-century British poetics would look rather different. (68)

2.3. Angela Carter

Angela Olive Pearce, best-known by the name under which she published her literature, Angela Carter, is regarded as "one of the boldest and most original writers of the 20th century.

Her work draws on an eclectic range of themes and influences, from gothic fantasy, traditional fairy tales, Shakespeare and music hall, through Surrealism and the cinema of Godard and Fellini" (British Library). Carter is regarded as a writer whose work "breaks many long-established taboos and mores, not least in her forthright realigning of women as central to, and in control of, their own narratives" (British Library).

Angela was born in 1940 in Eastbourne, England, and was the daughter of Hugh Alexander Stalker and Sophia Olive. Some aspects to highlight from Carter's childhood are the fact that she spent a great part of it with her grandmother in Yorkshire due to the bombing of the war, and that her first contact with cinema took place as a child. Since an early age, she loved films, and the seventh art would later prove influential in her career. Once she leaves school, in 1959, Angela starts working as a junior reporter in the *Croydon Advertiser,* and a year after she marries Paul Carter and moves to Bristol, where she studies Medieval Literature at University of Bristol (British Library). Then, it is in 1966 when Carter publishes her first novel *Shadow Dance*, and in the same decade she also writes *The Magic Toyshop* (1967) and *Several Perceptions* (1968). In fact, the 60s are a period for Carter in which she is "[h]eavily imbued with elements of gothic fantasy and horror, these early novels are also shot through with the libertarian energy of the 1960s" (British Library). Moreover, in 1967 and 1968 she wins two prizes for her novels, the John Llewellyn Rhys prize for *Magic Toyshop* and the Somerset Maugham Award for *Several Perceptions* respectively. What is more, in 1967 Angela also started writing essays for the magazine *New Society*, with which she collaborated for 20 years. Afterwards, in 1969 she travels to Japan since the condition of the Somerset Maugham Award was to "be used for foreign travel" (British Library). In this way, from 1969 to 1972 she lives in Japan, being Japanese culture highly influential for Carter. During this period of time, she works "briefly for NHK Broadcasting Company; sending articles back to *New Society*" (Sage ix). Then, in 1972 she divorces from Paul Carter and in the mid-70s she settles in London where she starts a relationship with Mark Pearce, having a child with him in 1983, named Alexander. "During the late 1970s and 80s, Carter taught at a number of universities; including Sheffield and East Anglia in Britain, Brown in the US and the University of Adelaide in Australia" (British Library). Furthermore, her literary production was very prolific during this period of Angela's career. In the 70s and the 80s she published the novels *Heroes and Villains* (1969), *The Infernal Desire Machines of Dr Hoffman* (1972), the short stories *Fireworks* (1974), and the novel *The Passion of New Eve* (1977) and *The Sadeian Woman* (1979), being all of these books highly influenced by the time she lived in Japan. What is more, in 1979 Carter publishes *The Bloody Chamber*, which has been regarded as her most successful work, and afterwards she also writes *Nights at the Circus* (1984) and *Wise Children* (1991), her last novel, together with a collection of essays such as *Nothing Sacred* (1982), *Expletives Deleted* (1992) and *Shaking a Leg* (1997).

Regarding the importance of Angela Carter's literature, her work was also adapted into the silver screen. The film released in 1984, *The Company of Wolves*, was based on her most successful literary production *The Bloody Chamber* (1979), the former being and adaptation of the latter. Indeed, the script of the movie was co-written by Angela Carter and the film director Neil Jordan. In addition, Carter won the James Tait Black Memorial Prize with her novel *Nights at the Circus*, and in 2012 it "was declared the best book to have ever been awarded that prize" (British library).

Angela Carter died on 16th February 1992 from a lung cancer. Since the writer passed away her work began being more studied and researched, as well as the sales of her books increased. In short, "[h]er writing occupies a unique place in 20th century fiction, a place where myths around gender and sexuality are debunked and where not even the deepest darkest recesses of human imagination are off-limits" (British Library).

3

ANALYSIS: IS MOTHERHOOD AN *INSTITUTION* IN THE CHOSEN NARRATIVES?

Now, taking into account the theoretical framework and above-explained objectives, different fragments of the chosen works will be studied to answer the question this monograph poses, if, in Adrienne Rich's words, motherhood is constituted as an *institution* in these narratives. Firstly place, the plot of these books will be briefly explained and, afterwards, some of their fragments will be analysed in order to respond the aforesaid question and draw conclusions.

3.1. George Eliot: Patty and Milly Barton

3.1.1. *"The Sad Fortunes of the Reverend Amos Barton"*

"The Sad Fortunes of the Reverend Amos Barton", as it has been pointed out before, was the first fictional work that George Eliot wrote, and it belongs with other two novellas to Eliot's *Scenes of Clerical Life*, published in 1857. This story focuses on Reverend Amos Barton's life, a new curate in Shepperton's church who:

> [I]s destined to a life of loneliness after the death of his wife … Milly. Barton's mourning is intensified by his realization that he has neglected her in life, distracted as he was by the competing attentions of a Polish countess, who, as it turns

out, was neither Polish, nor exactly a countess" (McDonagh 50-51).

In short, and focusing on the characters of the mother and the daughter, Milly Barton or Mrs Barton is married to Reverend Amos Barton, with whom she had six children, being the eldest her daughter Patty.

Having summarized the plot, some fragments of this story will be analysed to establish if in this mother-daughter relationship motherhood is constituted as the *institution* Rich suggests in her work.

3.1.2. Analysis

First of all, this diegesis is set in the Victorian society of 19th century England, and being embedded in this social and patriarchal constructions its characters act according to such social standards and expectations. In this way, throughout the narrative Milly Barton constitutes an epitome of the ideal Victorian woman, already depicted in the theoretical framework. For instance, this is discerned in the following fragment:

> But about half-past five o'clock in the morning, if there were any angels watching round her bed—and angels might be glad of such an office— they saw Mrs Barton rise up quietly, careful not to disturb the slumbering Amos, who was snoring the snore of the just, light her candle, prop herself upright with the pillows, throw the warm shawl round her shoulders, and renew her attack on the heap of undarned stockings. (Eliot 37)

Thus, this excerpt is just one example of Milly Barton's hard work as a housewife; here it is described how she devotes herself to her domestic tasks, waking up early to begin to do them, without of course waking up her husband. Moreover, she is presented as staying on the *inside* and constantly taking care of her children and husband. For example, when Mr Barton orders his wife "Milly, some of these children must go away. I want to be quiet" (Eliot 53), this proves that Milly is the only one raising the children up and providing peace and comfort to her husband. Therefore, in Ruskin's words, previously cited, Milly represents a perfect Victorian wife, since, as this author states, "wherever a true wife comes … home is always round her" (159), and Milly is depicted as constantly taking care of her home and family, which are her only concerns in life. Hence, this implies that Milly fulfils the above-mentioned concept discussed by Woolf of the *Angel in the House*, due to the fact that, other than performing her gender, she is also described as sacrificing her health for her family up to the point of losing her own identity and adopting just the identity of a mother and a wife. In this way, this character corresponds to Woolf's descriptions of the *Angel in the House*: "She was utterly unselfish. She excelled in the difficult arts of family life. She sacrificed herself daily" (141), and "she never had a mind or a wish of her own, but preferred to sympathize always with the minds and wishes of others" (Woolf 141). Additionally, Milly is depicted as lovely, fair, gentle, and tender, as it is seen in the following excerpt: "She was a lovely woman—Mrs Amos Barton; a large, fair, gentle Madonna … with large, tender, short-sighted eyes" (Eliot 28). Then, in this way, her character and attributes also fit in the qualities of the *Angel in the House*, since Woolf pointed out that this means being "intensely sympathetic. She was immensely charming … Above all — I need not say it—she was pure" (141). In addition, she is called all along the narrative a "sweet mother" and is depicted as a loving mother whose love is everlasting and works hard every day out of love for her children and husband. Indeed, Milly incarnates the conventional conception of motherhood Rich discusses in her work. Thus, Mrs Barton represents what traditionally has been regarded as a "natural mother" (Rich 3), that is to say, "a person without further identity, one who can find her chief gratification in being all day with small children, living at a pace tuned to theirs" (Rich 3). Furthermore, her character also proves true the idea that "the isolation of mothers and children together in the home must be taken for granted" (Rich 3). Ultimately, the character of Milly Barton, using Butler's terminology, performs her gender to the fullest. Besides, her gender constrictions are shaped according to the sociohistorical context and mindset of her time, the Victorian England. Consequently, this implies that gender roles are designed under patriarchy and the *male gaze* of that time, which postulated a pure, obedient, loving mother and wife who remained in the domestic sphere as the mould where women had to fit in.

Hence, taking into account this 19th century English Victorian context, and being aware that Milly embodies the traditional idea of motherhood, the "natural mother" (Rich 3), and the ideal Victorian woman, that is, the *Angel in the House*, the following fragment is going to be analysed. So, it will be determined if the relationship of Milly Barton with her daughter Patty, "the nine-year-old Patty, the eldest child" (Eliot 37), constitutes an *institution* of patriarchy, as Rich poses. This fragment takes place at the end of the story and situates Milly in her deathbed after giving birth (to a premature baby who also dies) when she is being visited by her little children before she dies. Then, she expresses a particular concern that she wants to solve before passing away, and this one is related to her daughter Patty:

It seemed as if Milly had heard the little footsteps on the stairs, for when Amos entered her eyes were wide open, eagerly looking towards the door. They all stood by the bedside—Amos nearest to her, holding Chubby and Dickey. But she motioned for Patty to come first, and clasping the poor pale child by the hand, said,—"Patty, I'm going away from you. Love your papa. Comfort him; and take care of your little brothers and sisters. God will help you."
Patty stood perfectly quiet, and said, "Yes, mamma." (Eliot 135)

Thereby, this passage highlights Milly's biggest worry is having someone to replace her role in the house, and her duties as a mother and a wife once she is gone. This is the reason why she wants to talk firstly to her daughter Patty when her children enter the room. Therefore, this passage proves that Milly, by using her 9-year-old daughter Patty as a substitute for her figure and everything this entails, is constituting herself a "force of conservation of traditional values" (Hirsch 14) which is asking Patty, at a very young age, to assume. Hence, as Rich points out, this fragment shows how "it is the mother through whom patriarchy early teaches the small female her proper expectations" (Rich 250). For this reason, "The Sad Fortunes of the Reverend Amos Barton" and the relationship between mother and daughter presented in this narrative proves that in this work motherhood becomes an *institution*. This is due to the fact that the patriarchal values of society at that time are perpetuated from mother to daughter through a mother who is embedded in patriarchal norms already, as it has been mentioned before, and who handles such norms to her daughter, perpetuating these ones over time and generations. This is why motherhood in this diegesis can be read as "the institution, which aims at ensuring that … all women—shall remain under control" (Rich lxi). Then, the patriarchal values Patty is asked by her mother to continue are related to her gender, the domestic sphere, the love of the "natural mother" (Rich 3), and the ideal "female" traits described both by Ruskin and Woolf before.

In this way, when Mrs Barton says to her children "Patty will try to be your mamma when I am gone, my darlings. You will be good, and not vex her" (Eliot 135), her words confirm Rich's statement that "[m]ost women in history have become mothers without choice, and even greater number have lost their lives bringing life into the world" (lxi-lxii). Indeed, due to her social context, Patty is not left with any other option but the imposed motherhood Rich mentions, that she must face and assume. Furthermore, concerning the last part of this statement by Rich, Milly in fact dies after giving birth prematurely to her baby, hence, the aforesaid assertion becomes true in this story.

Furthermore, regarding the character of the daughter, Patty seems to resign to what her mother has made her new role and purpose in life, as it is shown in the above-cited fragment: "Patty stood perfectly quiet, and said, "Yes, mamma" (Eliot 135). In addition, later in this episode, when they are leaving her mother, Patty wants to stay but ends up showing again an obedient attitude, as this passage exemplifies:

> Then Mrs Hackit and Nanny took them all away. Patty at first begged to stay at home and not go to Mrs Bond's again; but when Nanny reminded her that she had better go to take care of the younger ones, she submitted at once, and they were all packed in the ponycarriage once more. (Eliot 136)

Thereby, the daughter does not reject her mother's wishes by disagreeing or shows any attitude which could be related to the concept of *matrophobia*, cited above in the theoretical framework, like the protagonist of the following narrative to be analysed, *The Bell Jar*, does. On the contrary, Patty "stood perfectly quiet" (Eliot 135) and "submitted at once" (Eliot 136) to her mother's last wish of replacing her figure in the household and in the family. Then, the daughter in this diegesis performs her gender to the maximum as well as her mother, since she shows this mild, subdued, and obedient attitude expected from Victorian women. Patty is conscious of her context and thinks and feels what her mother asks her, substituting her, even if she is 9 years old, is her obligation, since a home could not be left without a woman to take care of the husband, children, and the household in the Victorian era. In short, when Patty agrees to replace her mother, she accomplishes the "conventional constructions of femininity" (Hirsch 12) of the Victorian period, "succumb[s] to convention" (Hirsch 11), like Milly, and becomes another *Angel in the House*. In this way, there is a double repetition, on the one hand regarding *gender performativity*, since Patty's "identity [is] instituted through a stylized repetition of acts" (Butler 519) just like her mom's. This means that both their identities are shaped by their gender roles, which are styled according to patriarchy's *male gaze*, and which they perform and accomplish through repetition, fitting in the role of the perfect Victorian wife and loving mother. Besides, on the other hand, the second repetition is regarding maternity, since in "The Sad Fortunes of the Reverend Amos Barton" motherhood becomes "a pattern of repetition from which [the daughter] cannot emerge and which precludes further development and progression" (Hirsch 21).

Finally, through the repetition of gender roles on both character's sides and the replacement of the mother by the daughter, as the fragments chosen and their analysis prove, in this narrative motherhood is constituted as the *institution* Rich claims. In this way, throughout this *institution* patriarchal values are repeated and therefore perpetuated from Milly to Patty Barton.

3.2. Sylvia Plath: Esther and Mrs Greenwood

3.2.1. *The* Bell Jar

Next, the plot of Plath's novel *The Bell Jar* (1963) will be explained to provide a context for the following analysis on how motherhood works in this piece of prose. This narrative is set in 1953 United States and its protagonist is Esther Greenwood, a middle-class undergraduate student who has just arrived in New York City. Esther, who is nineteen years old, has won a scholarship to Smith College, which is why she finds herself in New York, to work in a fashion magazine as a guest editor. During the period of time her scholarship lasts, Esther suffers from anxiety and finally goes back home to carry on with her studies. Throughout the story the protagonist experiences different episodes characterised by anxiety and depression, which will lead her eventually to an attempt to commit suicide, which results in her hospitalisation in an asylum. Esther's life and story is determined by her ability or inability to choose among the different paths she wants to follow, as it will be explained in depth in the analysis, which will be limited by society. Essentially social and gender constrictions are represented in the novel through her mother, Mrs Greenwood, her boyfriend, Buddy Willard, and his mother, Mrs Willard, who pushes Esther to be pure and to become a mother and a housewife, which clashes with her will of having a professional career and becoming a poet.

In short, *The Bell Jar*, which, as it has been highlighted before in Plath's biography, includes autobiographical tints, constitutes a narrative which discusses "an allegory about femininity, specifically 'the woman's place in society; her special creative powers; and finally, her psychological experience'" (Badia 131).

3.2.2. Analysis

Then, the plot of this narrative and its sociohistorical context, that is, the decade of the 50s in the USA marked by "Cold War politics, suburban structures and normative heterosexuality" (Badia 131), explains some of the character's behaviour. Thus, even if a century has passed since the women George Eliot wrote about, analysed above, and the gender roles which constricted them, in fact, these did not change much in the 1950s. In this way, even though during World War II women took on "men's jobs" while they were fighting, as the American icon *Rosie the Riveter* embodies, when the conflict was over certain ambiguity remained regarding the role women had to play. Hence, concerning Butler's concept of *gender performativity* cited above, the figure of the dream wife and ideal mother prevails still in the 50s, as the character of Buddy Willard's mother demonstrates. For example, once Mrs Willard gets married, she dedicates herself fully to the household, as the following fragment shows, when Esther reflects upon the possibility of getting married: "This seemed a dreary and wasted life for a girl with fifteen years of straight A's, but I knew what marriage was like, because cook and clean and wash was just what Buddy Willard's mother did from morning till night, and she was the wife of a university professor and had been a private school teacher herself" (Plath 80). Thereby, this excerpt proves that Mrs Willard did "succumb to convention" (Hirsch 11) and adjusts to the gender and "conventional constructions of femininity" (Hirsch 12) of her time by remaining in the domestic sphere. Thus, even though she had a job as a teacher, once she becomes a wife, she commits herself to the household chores, as Esther explains in this passage, sacrificing herself like Victorian women and the *Angel in the House*, who "sacrificed herself daily" (Woolf 141) for her family, did. Then, Mrs Willard demonstrates she is, in Ruskin's word's, a true wife according to patriarchal values, since "wherever a true wife comes, this home is always round her" (159). Thereby, Rich's statement, cited above, that "under patriarchy, female possibility has been literally massacred on the site of motherhood" (lxi-lxii) proves true in the figure of Mrs Willard, since she was once a school teacher but believes when becoming a wife and a mother that her place has to be on the *inside*, in the domestic sphere. In this way, using Butler's terminology, Buddy's mother acts performing her gender, because she behaves according to what is expected from her as a woman in the 50s, that is, to fit in the passive stereotyped mould created by patriarchy to preserve the power in male hands. Esther is expected to fit in such mould as well and, in fact, this is highlighted through Buddy Willard, who insists on the idea of motherhood:

> I also remembered Buddy Willard saying in a sinister, knowing way that after I had children I would feel differently, I wouldn't want to write poems any more. So I began to think maybe it was true that when you were married and had children it was like being brainwashed, and afterwards you went about numb as a slave in some private, totalitarian state. (Plath 81)

Accordingly, this excerpt shows how Buddy expects Esther to become a mother, which, again, demonstrates the gender expectations in the 50s regarding women. Hence, Esther is asked to become another *Angel in the House*, like Patty

Barton. Besides, he suggests that once Esther has children, she would not want to write more poetry. Therefore, this implies that Buddy has a conception of motherhood which lies on "unexamined assumptions" (Rich 3), presuming that "a 'natural' mother is a person without further identity, one who can find her chief gratification in being all day with small children" (Rich 3). Consequently, Buddy thinks Esther will replicate this role of a mother without no other identity than being a mother, and will lose her identity as a student, poet, editor, and so on, because this is what his mother, who lost her identity as a school teacher for maternity, incarnates. Buddy has interiorised such perception of women as having a singular identity as wives and mothers also due to the fact that it was normalized in the 50s and because traditionally "[w]oman's status as a childbearer has been made into a major fact of her life" (Rich lx). Therefore, this idea that Esther will lose her identity as a poet for maternity (like Mrs Willard did) proves that, then, "under patriarchy, female possibility [is] literally massacred on the site of motherhood" (Rich lxilxii), since motherhood is presented as an occupation to which women dedicate fully, without further personal goals, such as becoming a writer in the case of Esther, or having time of one's own. Thereby, Buddy hints at the idea of "motherhood as a single-minded identity" (Rich 7), which reduces women's identity to that of a mother or a wife only, which constitutes motherhood as "the institution, which aims at ensuring that [women's] potential—an all women—shall remain under control" (Rich lxi).

On the other hand, afterwards in Chapter 8, Buddy asks Esther if she wants to get married with him and the protagonist answers "I'm never going to get married" (Plath 89), to which Buddy replies with the following answer: "'You're crazy.' Buddy brightened. 'You'll change your mind'"

(Plath 89). Indeed, Buddy's answer, who cannot accept that a woman does not want to marry, portrays again the gender constrictions women had to face in the 50s, which are not far from those in the Victorian era in a certain way. What is more, the main character is called neurotic when she suggests that she does not want to choose between two things but rather have the two of them: "If neurotic is wanting two mutually exclusive things at one and the same time, then I'm neurotic as hell" (Plath 89-90). This can be understood as choosing to be a mother but also having a profession. In fact, Esther would like to choose different paths, but this looks like something unconceivable for her society. Nonetheless, after World War II, women started to enter little by little the labour market having professions which were regarded as "female jobs", such as being a teacher, nurse, or a secretary. However, it was thought that women had to follow one path in the 50s, preferably that of motherhood and marriage. This is exemplified when Esther explains her mixed feelings on choosing among her possibilities in the following excerpt, where the protagonist talks about a fig tree which works as an allegory of the different paths she could or would like to follow:

> From the tip of every branch, like a fat purple fig, a wonderful future beckoned and winked. One fig was a husband and a happy home and children, and another fig was a famous poet and another fig was a brilliant professor, and another fig was Ee Gee, the amazing editor … I saw myself sitting in the crotch of this fig tree, starving to death, just because I couldn't make up my mind which of the figs I would choose. I wanted each and every one of them, but choosing one meant losing all the rest, and, as I sat there, unable to decide, the figs began to wrinkle and go black, and, one by one, they plopped to the ground at my feet. (Plath 73)

Consequently, this passage shows beyond doubt that in Esther's society women normally could not follow more than one path simultaneously, since "choosing one meant losing all the rest" (Plath 73), and rather had to adjust to one, mostly maternity and marriage. Then, even if the social and historical context has changed from that of the previously analysed narrative, set in the Victorian era, these excerpts demonstrate how still in the 50s motherhood and the domestic sphere are preferred in the eyes of society when it comes to women. So, this envisages that the "force of conservation of traditional values" (Hirsch 14) is preserved throughout generations presumably thanks to *gender performativity* and the institutionalisation of motherhood, which have helped to preserve patriarchal thoughts. This implies that conventions are kept through repetition in this story too, like Mrs Willard embodies and Buddy's words reverberate regarding the Victorian conception of the ideal femininity, linked to maternity and the *inside*.

In this way, the aforementioned fragments from *The Bell Jar*, which portray women's situation in the 50s, are important when studying Esther's relationship with her mother. So far, it can be argued that motherhood constitutes an *institution* which perpetuates patriarchal values in this novel. Nevertheless, interestingly, motherhood is already presented as such *institution* through secondary characters, Bully Willard and his mother, Mrs Willard. However, the relationship between Esther and her mother is far more complex than that of Milly and Patty Barton, where the institutionalisation of motherhood is made clear. Meanwhile, in the case of Mrs Greenwood, her position is more ambiguous. First of all, Esther's mother, unlike Mrs Willard, keeps her job, and, what is more, her husband dies and she does not even mourn him, something that does not fit in the image of the ideal wife, like these excerpts show: "I had always been my father's favourite, and it seemed fitting I should take on a mourning my mother had never bothered with" (Plath 159); "[t]hen I remembered I had never cried for my father's death. My mother hadn't cried either. She had just smiled and said what a merciful thing it was for him that he died…" (Plath 161).

However, the figure of Mrs Greenwood is ambiguous because she does not embody a fully modern independent woman either, and she is described by Esther as being relegated to the domestic sphere once she gets married:

> Hadn't my own mother told me that as soon as she and my father left Reno on their honeymoon—my father had been married before, so he needed a divorce—my father said to her, 'Whew, that's a relief, now we can stop pretending and be ourselves?' and from that day on my mother never had a minute's peace. (Plath 80-81)

Hence, this fragment proves that Mrs Greenwood "succumb[s] to convention" (Hirsch 11) by becoming a wife and a mother, performing her gender according to the patriarchal values shaped by the *male gaze*. Then, since she "never had a minute's peace" (Plath 80-81) when she marriages, this quality of sacrificing for others and not having time of one's own aligns with Mrs Willard and the *Angel in the House* mentioned above, who "sacrificed herself daily" (Woolf 141) for her family. Thereby, the character of Mrs Greenwood also proves true that "motherhood as an institution has ghettoized and degraded female potentialities" (Rich lxi), since once she marries, her life is limited, and she does not enjoy free time anymore. Therefore, this also confirms again Rich's statement that "under patriarchy, female possibility has been literally massacred on the site of motherhood" (lxi-lxii). Nonetheless, even if Mrs Greenwood "succumb[s] to convention" (Hirsch 11), she does not completely reject modernity either, as she works at a college, like Esther points out:

> So I looked up the requirements for English majors at the city college where my mother taught ... This surprised me. I had always looked down on my mother's college, as it was co-ed, and filled with people who couldn't get scholarships ... Now I saw the stupidest person at my mother's college knew more than I did. (Plath 120121)

Then, the character of Esther's mother does not renounce to having a plural identity once she becomes a mother, since she is also a teacher, though her life is marked by the event of having a family, which limits her: "[M]y mother never had a minute's peace" (Plath 8081). Hence, Mrs Greenwood portrays the duality women started to face in the 50s, when, as it has been proved throughout Buddy Willard and Mrs Willard, society still preferred women who remained in the domestic sphere dedicating their lives to their families, but social changes started to occur as women began entering the labour market as well. Thus, it can be argued that Esther's mother becomes a starting bridge from tradition to modernity. However, she occupies a "female job" and still defends conventions, which is why she can be read as a bridge towards change which has not yet arrived to the other side. In this way, even if Mrs Greenwood accomplishes some of the new changes of her society, by having her own job, she still preserves rooted ideas regarding womanhood, since she has been raised up and embedded in a patriarchal society shaped by conventions and tradition. For instance, Esther's mother tries to instil the traditional ideas of her time regarding sexuality in her daughter, who states that "[w]hen I was nineteen, pureness was the great issue" (Plath

77), as the following passage shows: "My mother had always told me never under any circumstances to go with a man to a man's room after an evening out, it could mean only the one thing" (Plath 76). What is more, Mrs Greenwood cut an article from a magazine which "gave all the reasons a girl shouldn't sleep with anybody but her husband" (Plath 76) and mailed it to Esther at college. While the protagonist narrates this event, she explains that the article's point was that men's and women's emotions were different and that:

> Only marriage can bring the two worlds and the two different sets of emotions together properly. My mother said this was something a girl didn't know about till it was too late, so she had to take the advice of people who were already experts, like a married woman. (Plath 76-77)

Nevertheless, Esther does not follow her mother's advice and goes to a man's room: "When Constantin asked if I would like to come up to his apartment ... I smiled to myself" (Plath 76). In fact, she rejects her mother's conventional mindset, which regarding women and purity is very similar to the Victorian one, since Woolf depicts the *Angel in the House*, like it has been previously quoted, as a woman who "[a]bove all — I need not say it—she was pure" (141). Furthermore, Esther's rejection of traditional ideas regarding sex is pointed out in this passage: "I couldn't stand the idea of a woman having to have a simple pure life and a man being able to have a double life, one pure and one not" (Plath 77). Thereby, this fragment shows that Esther is critical, has her own ideas, and is conscious of the social conventions her mother supports and she rejects. Hence, there is a clash between the mindset of two different generations, the mother's and the daughter's. Moreover, regarding these narrow-minded thoughts on women's sexuality and Esther's refusal of such, the main character makes her own decision, disagreeing with her mother, by going to a doctor and getting a diaphragm fitted. This event is described as a conquer of her own freedom: "I climbed up on the examination table thinking: I am climbing to my freedom, freedom from fear, from marrying the wrong person, like Buddy Willard, just because of sex" (Plath 213). In addition, once Esther gets the diaphragm, she states owning herself and her identity, and she asserts: "I was my own woman" (Plath 213).

Besides, there is another clash between mother and daughter concerning Esther's future job, as this fragment poses:

> My mother kept telling me nobody wanted a plain English major. But an English major who knew shorthand was something else again. Everybody would want her. She would be in demand among all the up-and-coming young men and she would transcribe letter after thrilling letter. The trouble was, I hated the idea of serving men in any way. I wanted to dictate my own thrilling letters. (Plath 72)

Therefore, in Woolf words, Mrs Greenwood proposes Esther a profession (which fits in what were regarded as "female jobs" in the 50s) in which she would not have "a mind of her own" (141), and whose work would be subordinated to that of men's. Then, she would just transcribe, repeating men's words, while they would be regarded then as "eminently the doer, the creator" (Ruskin 158). Meanwhile, Esther declares that she wants to write, not copy somebody's writing; she has and wants to make use of "a mind of her own" (141): "I hated the idea of serving men in any way. I wanted to dictate my own thrilling letters" (Plath 72). Accordingly, in this excerpt, as well as in the previous one when Esther exerts her sexual freedom by getting a diaphragm, the main character proves to have this "mind of her own" (Woolf 141) and to be critical, unlike Patty Barton in the narrative analysed before. Thus, in contrast to Patty, who is subdued and takes on her mother's role, Esther shows a rejection of her mother's ideals and wishes and wants to have her own thoughts and identity. Therefore, *matrophobia,* meaning "the fear not of one's mother but of *becoming one's mother"* (Rich 240), is found in the relationship between Esther and Mrs Greenwood, since the daughter does not want to follow the path of repetition her mother suggests and incarnates.

Moreover, concerning this generational mindset difference, Mrs Greenwood also embodies the aspect of traditional motherhood related to the concept of blame explained above in the theoretical framework. For instance, after Esther attempts to commit suicide and is hospitalised in an asylum, her mother asks her daughter the following question: "My mother was the worst. She never scolded me, but kept begging me, with a sorrowful face, to tell her what she had done wrong" (Plath 195). Therefore, this fragment demonstrates that Esther's mother feels she has done something wrong and blames herself because of her daughter's state, since she feels she has failed, in society's eyes, as a mother, becoming the so-called "bad mother". Besides, Esther is conscious of her mother's feelings: "My mother's face floated to my mind, a pale reproachful moon, at her last and first visit to the asylum since my twentieth birthday. A daughter in an asylum! I had done that to her. Still, she had obviously decided to forgive me" (Plath 226-227). Accordingly, this passage proves as well that Mrs Greenwood has the traits of the "'natural' mother" (Rich 3), that is, the conventional mother who shows everlasting love, embodying "the stereotype of the mother whose love is 'unconditional'" (Rich 7).

In short, motherhood is presented as an *institution* in this narrative and not only through the character of the protagonist's mother. On the one hand, the characters of Buddy Willard and Mrs Willard, as the previous fragments show, describe the mould in which women had to fit in accordance with gender roles in the 50s, which in a certain way is not far from the Victorian one. Thus, Mrs Willard portrays the traditional woman and Buddy echoes these conventions since he wants Esther to follow the path of marriage and motherhood. Nevertheless, the protagonist of *The Bell Jar* wants to have a plural identity and considers that maternity and the domestic sphere, in Esther's words, mean "being brainwashed" (Plath 81) and imply:

> [G]etting up at seven and cooking him eggs and bacon and toast and coffee and dawdling about in my nightgown and curlers after he'd left for work to wash up the dirty plates and make the bed, and then when he came home after a lively, fascinating day he'd expect a big dinner, and I'd spend the evening washing up even more dirty plates till I fell into bed, utterly exhausted. (Plath 80)

On the other hand, concerning the figure of Esther's mother, motherhood is also used as an institutionalized tool of patriarchy to instil conservative ideas from mothers in daughters, as the passages analysed above regarding sexuality, pureness and the job as a stenographer prove. Consequently, the mother in this story, together with the other characters, is "through whom patriarchy early teaches the small female her proper expectations" (Rich 250). Nonetheless, unlike the previously studied mother-daughter relationship, that of Milly and Patty Barton, Esther shows a behaviour related to *matrophobia* and rejects her mother's narrow-minded thoughts. Then, unlike in the previous narrative, there is a generational clash and Esther wants to break with the "pattern of repetition from which she cannot emerge and which precludes further development and progression" (Hirsch 21) that defines the relationship with her mother. Hence, *matrophobia* in Plath's novel can be understood as "a womanly splitting of the self, in the desire to become purged once and for all of our mothers' bondage, to become individual and free" (Rich 242). For example, Esther pursues and accomplishes this when she gets a diaphragm or asserts she does not want to repeat men's writing as a stenographer but to write her own words. Hence, Esther wants to break with the social pattern of repetition, she wants to write and create not to transcribe and repeat, like the passage of the rejection to work as a shorthand shows, working as a metaphor of her refusal to repeat standards in general.

Finally, even if Mrs Greenwood and Esther's relationship is not as categorical as that of Milly and Patty Barton, motherhood and the mother in *The Bell Jar*, as well as characters such as Buddy and Mrs Willard demonstrate, prove true Rich's statement on how literary images help perpetuating this conventional vision of motherhood through "the visual and literary images of motherhood as a single-minded identity" (7). In this way, the reminiscence of such traditional thoughts coming from the Victorian times in this story set in the 50s, other than being perpetuating through society, its "stylized repetition of acts" (Butler 519), *gender performativity*, and motherhood, ultimately through repetition; are preserved as well by means of literature, which at the end is influenced by the society of its context. This is definitely seen in Plath's novel when Esther claims: "I remember a worrisome course Victorian novel where woman after woman died, palely and nobly, in torrents of blood, after a difficult childbirth" (Plath 221), which very much describes Milly Barton's end. Therefore, as the title of the novel anticipates in the form of a prolepsis, women in it, as well as the characters of Eliot's work analysed above, are trapped in a bell jar, that is, society's expectations according to their gender which limits their identities, and which Esther tries to break by pursuing a "singularity based on disidentification from the fate of other women, especially mothers" (Hirsch 10).

3.3. Angela Carter: the Daughter and the Mother in a New Perception of Motherhood

3.3.1. "The Bloody Chamber"

Last but not least, motherhood in Angela Carter's collection of short stories compiled into *The Bloody Chamber and Other Stories* published in 1979 is going to be discussed. This work is a feminist rewriting of different traditional fairy tales including the following fictions: "The Bloody Chamber", "The Courtship of Mr Lyon", "The Tiger's Bride", "Puss-in-Boots", "The Erl-King", "The Snow Child", "The Lady of the House of Love", "The Werewolf", "The Company of Wolves", and "Wolf-Alice".

This monograph focuses on the mother-daughter relationship in "The Bloody Chamber", which is based on "Bluebeard". Thus, in the first place, the plot of the latter will be briefly explained in order to understand the changes made by Carter in the former. On the one hand, "Bluebeard" is a story belonging to French folklore which was included in Charles Perrault's *Histoires ou contes du temps passé* (1697). In this folk tale Bluebeard is a wealthy man belonging to the nobility who has married six times, but whose wives have disappeared mysteriously. Then, as he wants to marry again, he visits his neighbour to marry one of his daughters and finally makes the youngest his wife, which terrifies her family who is aware of how Bluebeard's previous marriages ended. Thus, when this young lady moves with him to his palace in the countryside, he suddenly tells her that he has to leave for some days and gives her the keys of the palace on the condition that she will not enter a chamber which is situated underground. While Bluebeard is away, the young woman invites her sister Anne, and some friends and family to the palace. Finally, she succumbs to her curiosity and goes inside the forbidden chamber in which she finds Bluebeard's six previous wives murdered and rivers of blood. Frightened, she drops the key which gets stained with blood. Later, she tries to clean it but since this key has magical properties the blood does not get removed. Then, out of the sudden Bluebeard comes back and finds out what her wife has done and thinks about killing her *ipso facto*, but he reconsiders this and lets her pray for the last time with Anne. Finally, when he is about to kill his wife, her brothers arrive and kill Bluebeard. In this way, the young lady buries the murdered wives and inherits his husband's palace and fortune, which is used to get her siblings married and remarry herself again.

On the other hand, in Angela Carter's "The Bloody Chamber", which is very similar to its hypotext but introduces new changes and perspectives, the main character is a teenager who marries a French Marquis, who, like Bluebeard, has married before, in this case three times, and whose previous wives have vanished. Thus, she leaves her mother and her home and moves with him to his castle in Brittany. Then, in the same way as Bluebeard, the Marquis has to leave to attend some business and leaves his wife the keys of the castle, warning her that it is forbidden to go to a certain chamber. While the girl is alone, as she is a pianist, she grows fond of a new character introduced by Carter, a blind piano tuner. In the end, like in the hypotext of "Bluebeard", she succumbs to curiosity and goes into the prohibited chamber after discovering some documents related to the Marquis' ex-wives. In this way, she finds these women murdered inside this room in different horrifying ways and terrified she drops they key which gets stained with blood. Afterwards, she tells about her discovering to the piano tuner, but the Marquis suddenly comes back and finds out everything. Then, he presses the stained key against the young girl's forehead leaving a red mark on her that will last forever. Finally, when the Marquis is about to behead the girl, while the blind piano tuner is unable to save her, her mother appears shooting the villain, killing him, and saving her daughter. At the end of the story, the money she inherits is destined to charities and the castle is turned into a school for blind people, as well as the three characters move together, and the protagonist establishes a music school in Paris.

Now, after having briefly explained the plot of "The Bloody Chamber" and shown its main differences regarding the folktale of "Bluebeard", since it entails more details and interesting aspects that could be analysed in relation to the Marquis and his relationship with the protagonist, the mother-daughter relationship in this fiction is going to be analysed. Indeed, motherhood proves to be an essential change in regard to the hypotext on which Carter based this narrative.

3.3.2. Analysis

Then, as well as in the previous narratives, the context in which this short story is written has to be taken into account, that is, the end of the 70s. This decade is characterised by the second wave of feminism, which was very much concerned with family, domesticity, reproductive rights, and so on, proposing a critique of the patriarchal male-dominated society, world, and institutions.

Thus, Carter's plot demonstrates, as the mother is the one who saves the daughter, that the former embodies a very different character in comparison to the mother in "The Sad Fortunes of the Reverend Amos Barton" and *The Bell Jar*. In this way, the mother of the protagonist of "The Bloody Chamber" plays an active role while George Eliot's Milly Barton is completely passive or Plath's Mrs Greenwood constitutes a new form of the *Angel in the House*; since even if she has a job as a teacher (a "female job"), she keeps being subdued to the domestic realm and society's expectations, as it was shown above in the previous analysis.

What is more, concerning marriage, which has been very present in Western literary tradition when it comes to the mother-daughter relationship, as it is discerned in Jane Austen's works for instance—and which was a big concern still in the society of Esther Greenwood in the 50s—in this narrative the mother's attitude towards this one proves different. In this way, in "The Bloody Chamber" the mother is reluctant to her daughter's marriage, and she even asks her if she loves the man she is about to get married with: "Are you sure you love him?" (Carter 7). Therefore, instead of being happy because her daughter is following society's expectations by marrying, which implies "succumb[ing] to convention" (Hirsch 11), and fitting in the "conventional constructions of femininity" (Hirsch 12), the mother is uneasy. Hence, the mother of this fiction behaves unlike previous mothers in literature, since Milly Barton or Mrs Greenwood, for example, would probably have shown a more positive attitude towards their daughter's marriage. However, on the contrary, Carter's mother in this fiction shows a different point of view: "my mother had been reluctant to see her girl whisked off by a man so recently bereaved" (Carter 10).

Besides, in this tale the daughter admires her mother and regards her as a role model. Unlike Esther Greenwood, who rejects becoming her mother since she embodies tradition, the mother in Carter's narrative is attributed positive traits which the daughter praises, as it is seen in the following fragment:

> My eagle-featured, indomitable mother; what other student at the Conservatoire could boast that her mother had outfaced a junkful of Chinese pirates, nursed a village through a visitation of the plague, shot a man-eating tiger with her own hand and all before she was as old as I?". (Carter 7)

Consequently, this excerpt demonstrates how instead of rejecting her mother the protagonist boasts about her. In addition, in this story, the mother is not depicted as a subdued or mild character anymore, but as a strong, active, brave, adventurous, and "indomitable" (Carter 7) woman. Moreover, as the following passages show, the daughter embraces the influence of her mother's character on her:

> Until that moment, this spoiled child did not know she had inherited nerves and a will from the mother who had defied the yellow outlaws of Indo-China; My mother's spirit drove me on, into that dreadful place, in a cold ecstasy to know the very worst. (Carter 28)

Accordingly, this statement shows how, unlike Esther Greenwood, the protagonist does not reject the traits she has inherited from her mother, but celebrates them. Therefore, it can be argued that, contrary to the previous analysed narrative, in this mother-daughter relationship there are no signs of *matrophobia*. Additionally, even if the main character's mother disapproves of her daughter's decision of marrying, the protagonist does not reject her or describes her mother through negative adjectives, but keeps praising her.

Furthermore, the mother ends up being the heroine of this story, the saviour of her daughter. Unlike traditional folk tales where male characters are presented as the rescuers of the so-called damsel in distress—like the brothers of the main character do in the original tale of "Bluebeard"—Carter changes the perspective in her rewriting of this story, designing a mother character who takes on the active role of the rescuer. For instance, this fragment right before the villain of the tale, the Marquis, is killed, summarises the active role the figure of the mother plays in this story:

> You never saw such a wild thing as my mother, her hat seized by the winds and blown out to sea so that her hair was her white mane, her black lisle legs exposed to the thigh, her skirts tucked round her waist, one hand on the reins of the rearing horse while the other clasped my father's service revolver and, behind her, the breakers of the savage, indifferent sea, like the witnesses of a furious justice. And my husband stood stock-still, as if she had been Medusa, the sword still raised over his head as in those clockwork tableaux of Bluebeard that you see in glass cases at fairs ... Now, without a moment's hesitation, she raised my father's gun, took aim and put a single, irreproachable bullet though my husband's head. (Carter 43-44)

Hence, in this excerpt, in which there is a direct reference to "Bluebeard", the mother's protagonist is depicted again as a figure of freedom and independence, describing her through adjectives such as "wild" (Carter 43) and comparing her to Medusa. This simile to the Greek character of Medusa, who can be read as a figure representing female anger and power, is interesting because it places the mother character in Carter's fiction, once more, at a distance from stereotypical subdued mother figures.

In short, the mother-daughter relationship in "The Bloody Chamber" does not entail motherhood as an *institution*, unlike the above-analysed relationships. Nonetheless, since this story is a revision and rewriting of a fairy tale, and it also breaks with the stereotypical relationship in Western literature between mothers and daughters; the rejection of such relationship implies the acceptance that traditionally maternity has been institutionalised in literature, in order to reject its institutionalisation. In other words, rewriting something implies the previous existence of the thing that is being rewritten. Thereby, the rewriting of this story changing the traditional mother-daughter relationship implies its previous institutionalisation and conception as a tool of patriarchy to perpetuate traditional values. Thus, the mother in the last analysed narrative, unlike the other two previous fictions, proves to incarnate the opposite to "ideal femininity" (Hirsch 14), to the conception of a "'natural' mother" (Rich 3) as "a person without further identity" (Rich 3), to the *Angel in the House*, and to Ruskin's ideal "true wife", whose "home is always round her" (Ruskin 159). What is more, this mother does not follow society's "unexamined assumptions" (Rich 3) regarding motherhood. Additionally, these facts are shown throughout her daughter's words mentioned above, which depict her mother as an "indomitable mother" (Carter 7) who is wild: "You never saw such a wild thing as my mother" (Carter 43). Furthermore, she is also described as being brave and adventurous, since she "had outfaced a junkful of Chinese pirates, nursed a village through a visitation of the plague, shot a man-eating tiger with her own hand" (Carter 7). Hence, this situates her outside the domestic realm and society's constrictions, regarding being a mother and a woman, who shaped by the *male gaze* tend to become passive and quiet women, such as Milly Barton. In addition, she takes on the role of the rescuer, traditionally embodied by male figures in literature, to save her daughter, which once more demonstrates that she plays an active and strong character, like the final analysed excerpt highlights: "[A]s if she had been Medusa, the sword still raised over his head ... Now, without a moment's hesitation, she raised my father's gun, took aim and put a single, irreproachable bullet though my husband's head" (Carter 43-44). Thereby, Carter's mother does not lose herself to motherhood (Biss xii), since she does not incarnates a "single-minded identity" (Rich 7), but a plural one, and has a "mind of her own" (Woolf 141), by taking on the role of the saviour, for example. Therefore, this mother does not embody for her daughter, like mothers have traditionally done, the "force of conservation of traditional values" (Hirsch 14), since she breaks with *gender performativity* and also disapproves of the fact that her daughter marriages so soon. Accordingly, and taking into account the previous analysed excerpts from "The Bloody Chamber", it can be concluded that in this narrative the mother does not suppose for the daughter "a pattern of repetition from which she cannot emerge, and which precludes further development and progression" (Hirsch 21). In fact, this mother herself breaks "the bell jar", which in summary is the "pattern of repetition" (Hirsch 21) which limits women's identity and possibilities, by behaving against society's expectations. Furthermore, the daughter in this narrative admires her mother and regards as positive the attributes she has inherited from her: "Until that moment, this spoiled child did not know she had inherited nerves and a will from the mother who had defied the yellow outlaws of Indo-China; My mother's spirit drove me on" (Carter 28). Hence, this excerpt demonstrates that there is no *matrophobia* or disidentification from the mother, who does not "become the target[s] of this process of disidentification and the primary negative model[s] for the daughter" (Hirsch 11) in this narrative. Accordingly, the mother in this short story by Carter does not imply a constriction on her daughter's identity, like in the previous narratives analysed above, but rather incarnates a model of "courageous mothering" (Rich 253), which becomes a role model and "illuminate[s] and expand[s] her [daughter's] sense of actual possibilities" (Rich 253).

4
CONCLUSIONS

The analysis of the excerpts studied above from the chosen narratives allows to answer the question this study poses, if motherhood constitutes a patriarchal, in Rich's words, *institution* in which mothers instil in daughters gender norms and society's expectations, perpetuating conventional patriarchal values throughout generations. Thus, the first story analysed, "The Sad Fortunes of Revered Amos Barton" by George Eliot, presents a mother-daughter relationship in which the mother completely embodies the patriarchal *institution* Rich highlights and that has been explained above. In this way, Milly Barton incarnates the ideal Victorian woman and the *Angel in the House*, a role which she leaves to her nine-year-old daughter Patty, whom she asks to replace her both as a mother and as a housewife, meaning, that the daughter possibilities get reduced to those the mother had, belonging these ones to the domestic sphere. Moreover, on the one hand, *The Bell Jar* by Sylvia Plath shows a mother-daughter relationship more ambiguous than the previous one. The mother in this story does not limit her daughter possibilities as directly as Milly Barton does, but still shows conservative and traditional ideas which she tries to instil in her daughter too. The ambiguity of this relationship is also seen through the figure of the mother herself who, although having a profession, is still highly linked to domesticity. In the end, motherhood portrays a patriarchal *institution* as well in this fiction, since even if the mother is ambiguous, she supports conventional patriarchal ideas and, what is more, other characters try to reduce the protagonist to the single identity of the mother and the housewife, which contradicts her desire to have a plural identity, as a poet for example. What is more, the daughter in this story, unlike the obedient daughter Patty Barton embodies, rejects becoming like his mother or incarnating society's conception of the ideal woman, since she is conscious of the limitations these would imply for her. Accordingly, in this relationship the concept of *matrophobia* is found and, the daughter even says that she hates her mother: "'I hate her,' I said, and waited for the blow to fall. But Doctor Nolan only smiled at me as if something had pleased her very, very much, and said, 'I suppose you do'" (Plath 195). Whereas, on the other hand, "The Bloody Chamber" by Angela Carter presents a mother-daughter relationship which breaks with the one presented in the previous narratives, since the mother is praised by the daughter. Moreover, this mother, who is depicted by her own daughter as indomitable, wild, brave, or adventurous, does not fulfil society's constrictions or performs according to her gender, nor does she ask her daughter to do so either. Thereby, motherhood is not imposed as a patriarchal *institution* in this short story, where the mother also embodies an active character who takes on the role of the rescuer of her daughter—an aspect which clashes with the conventional depiction of motherhood and the mother-daughter relationship in Western literary tradition.

In addition, these diegeses show the gender norms and the society of each of the periods when they were written, the English Victorian 19th century, the decade of the 50s the USA, and the 70s respectively. In this way, these fictions become "literary images of motherhood" (Rich 7), which are inspired by reality and the social context in which they are conceived. Then, their comparison shows different social changes, as it has been seen above in their analysis. In fact, this is one of the reasons why these narratives in particular were chosen to answer the goal of this monograph. Since these writers and stories have a different context, these particular fictions allow to discuss, on the one hand, a very passive mother role, through Milly Barton; on the other hand, an ambiguous motherhood influenced by the social changes women were facing in the 50s in the USA, *in The Bell Jar*; and, finally, a breaking conception of motherhood designed under the third wave of feminism, which is taking place when "The Bloody Chamber" is written. Therefore, it was considered that the comparison of these stories in particular will allow to comment on different types of mothers and mother-daughter relationships, and they were chosen carefully to present a study from a more limiting motherhood to a freer one. Furthermore, the comparison was thought important for the question this work poses, since it was considered that, by comparing different stories from different periods, it will be demonstrated as well if motherhood was such *institution* through generations. In this way, comparing narratives from different periods, it could be discerned if certain patriarchal values and gender prejudices were repeated in them, being then perpetuated, and turning motherhood, then, into an *institution*. In fact, this was proved in the analysis of *The Bell Jar* which, although is set in the 50s, shows a reminiscence of traditional ideas and patriarchal values which were already present in "The Sad Fortunes of the Reverend Amos Barton", set in the 19th century. Consequently, the comparison of these two works proves motherhood can be erected as *institution*, since the mother in the 50s repeats traditional ideas that date back from the 19th century, which she tries to instil in her daughter.

Then, the answers given to the question this research posed are achieved thanks to the accomplishment of the objectives set at the beginning of this work. Thus, the secondary objectives, from one to four, helped to back up with documentary evidence the main goals of this study, which are found in objective from five to nine. Hence, the theoretical framework and the biographies and literary production of the three authors—the secondary objectives— helped to carry out an in-depth analysis of the chosen works in order to contrast them and to draw conclusions from their study, achieving in this way the main objectives of this monograph.

Finally[3], due to the length this research was supposed to have, it was regarded that the comparison of these three narratives will permit the discussion of different types of motherhood through which the initial question in relation to its institutionalisation could be answered from different perspectives. Nevertheless, if this discussion was provided with more length, a greater number of fictions could be studied in order to revise the mother-daughter relationship and how it has been traditionally depicted in literature. What is more, maybe even a category of types of mothers and daughters could be discerned or created as a result of a bigger study.

───────────────

3   This monograph, being the result of an Undergraduate Thesis of the English Studies degree at University of Córdoba, followed the corresponding guidelines.

5
WORKS CITED

Adams, Alice. "Maternal Bonds: Recent Literature on Mothering." *Signs*, vol. 20, no. 2, 1995, pp. 414–27. *JSTOR*, http://www.jstor.org/stable/3174956. Accessed 19 Feb. 2023.

Badia, Janet. "The Bell Jar and Other Prose." *The Cambridge Companion to Sylvia Plath*, edited by Jo Gill, Cambridge University Press, 2006, pp. 124-38.

Bennett, Joan. *George Eliot: Her Mind and Her Art*. Cambridge University Press, 1966.

Biss, Eula. "Of Institution Born." *Of Woman Born: Motherhood as Experience and Institution*, by Adrienne Rich, W.W. Norton & Company, 2021, pp. xi-xx.

Bodenheimer, Rosemarie. "A Woman of Many Names." *The Cambridge Companion to George Eliot*, edited by George Levine, Cambridge University, 2001, pp. 20-37.

British Library. "Angela Carter." *British Library*, https://www.bl.uk/people/angela-carter. Accessed 17 Apr. 2023.

Bronfen, Elisabeth. *Sylvia Plath*. 2nd ed., Northcote House Pub Limited, 2004.

Butler, Judith. "Performative Acts and Gender Constitution: An Essay in Phenomenology and Feminist Theory." *Theatre Journal*, vol. 40, no. 4, 1988, pp. 51931. *JSTOR*, https://doi.org/10.2307/3207893. Accessed 10 Jan. 2023.

Cambridge Dictionary. "English Dictionary, Translations & Thesaurus." *Cambridge Dictionary*, dictionary. cambridge.org/. Accessed 19 Dec. 2023.

Carter, Angela. "The Bloody Chamber." *The Bloody Chamber and Other Stories*. Penguin, 2015, pp. 1-45.

Eliot, George. "The Sad Fortunes of the Reverend Amos Barton." *Scenes of Clerical Life: By George in Two Volumes*, edited by William Blackwood and Sons, vol. 1, London: William Blackwood and Sons, 1858, pp. 3-151. ProQuest, https://www.proquest.com/docview/2138577036/Z000036909/EE6C3ED250D24A27PQ/1?accountid=14520. Accessed 28 of Apr. 2023.

Enwistle, Alice. "Plath and Contemporary British Poetry." *The Cambridge Companion to Sylvia Plath*, edited by Jo Gill, Cambridge University Press, 2006, pp. 6370.

Ewaidat, Hala. "Reconstructing the Mother-Daughter Relationship: Lydia Davis and Amy Tan." *Arab World English Journal*, vol. 5, no. 1, 2021, pp. 324-35. *AWEJ for Translation & Literary Studies*, doi: http://dx.doi.org/10.24093/awejtls/vol5no1.22. Accessed 19 Feb. 2023.

Hirsch, Marianne. *The Mother/Daughter Plot: Narrative, Psychoanalysis, Feminism*. Indiana University Press, 1989.

McDonagh, Josephine. "The Early Novels." *The Cambridge Companion to George Eliot*, edited by George Levine, Cambridge University Press, 2001, pp. 38-56.

Mulvey, Laura. "Visual pleasure and narrative cinema." *Visual and other pleasures*. London: Palgrave Macmillan UK, 1989, pp. 14-26.

Noddings, Nel. *Caring: A Feminine Approach to Ethics & Moral Education*. University of California Press, 1984.

Patmore, Coventry. *The Angel in the House*. Cassell & Company, Limited: London, Paris & Melbourne, 1891. Project Gutenberg, 10 Aug. 2014, https://www.gutenberg.org/files/4099/4099-h/4099-h.htm. Accessed 22 Feb. 2023.

Plath, Sylvia. *The Bell Jar*. Faber and Faber, 2019.

Rich, Adrienne. *Of Woman Born: Motherhood as Experience and Institution*. W.W. Norton & Company, 2021.

Ruskin, John. "Of Queen's Garden." *Selected Writings*, edited by Dinah Birch, Oxford University Press, 2004, pp. 150-174.

Sage, Lorna. *Angela Carter*. 2nd ed., Northcote House Pub Limited, 2007.

Smith College. "Sylvia Plath Special Collections Resources: About Sylvia Plath." *Smith College*, 3 Feb. 2023, https://libguides.smith.edu/c.php?g=1227026&p=8978401. Accessed 14 Apr. 2023.

Wagner-Martin, Linda. "Plath and Contemporary American Poetry." *The Cambridge Companion to Sylvia Plath*, edited by Jo Gill, Cambridge University Press, 2006, pp. 52-62.

Woolf, Virginia. "Professions for Women." *Selected Essays*, edited by David Bradshaw, Oxford University Press, 2008, pp. 140-145.

6
ACKNOWLEDGEMENTS

To the University of Córdoba, for giving me the opportunity to study at the University of Limerick, Ireland, thanks to the Erasmus programme—an experience without which the two undergraduate theses of my double degree could not have been conceived.

To Sinéad McDermott, who teaches Contemporary Women's Writing at UL, for showing us female authors beyond the canon, modern works, topics, and theoretical concepts regarding women and literature.

To my friends I met in Limerick, with whom I discussed the books we read in Contemporary Women's Writing.

To Juan de Dios Torralbo Caballero, for helping me with this work and for being the first professor in my degree who introduced us to reading texts from a gender perspective.

To both professors, for demonstrating and transmitting the passion they have for literature and women's literary work, which has been very inspiring for me.

To my mom, who has always wanted me to become an independent woman since my childhood.